ACHINES AT WORK

rs

Clive Gifford

WAYLAND

Published in 2013 by Wayland
Copyright © Wayland 2013

Wayland
338 Euston Road
London NW1 3BH

Wayland Australia
Level 17/207 Kent Street
Sydney, NSW 2000

Editor: Nicola Edwards
Designer: Elaine Wilkinson
Picture Researcher: Clive Gifford

British Library Cataloguing in Publication
Data

Gifford, Clive.
    Cars. -- (Machines at work)
    1. Automobiles--Juvenile literature.
    I. Title II. Series
    629.2'22-dc23

ISBN: 978 0 7502 7808 9

10 9 8 7 6 5 4 3 2

Printed in China
Wayland is a division of Hachette Children's
Books, an Hachette UK company

www.hachette.co.uk

To find out about the author, visit his website:
www.clivegifford.co.uk

Picture acknowledgements:
The author and publisher would like to thank
the following agencies and people for allowing
these pictures to be reproduced:
Cover (main) Max Earey / Shutterstock.
com, (inset) Calvin Chan / Shutterstock.com;
title page 3777190317 / Shutterstock.com;
pp2-3 SÃ¡gi ElemÃ©r / Shutterstock.com;
p4 Shutterstock © Ben Smith; p5 (t) iStock
© Ivan Cholakov, (b) iStock © Caboclin; p6
© George Tiedemann/GT Images/Corbis;
p7 iStock © Lisa Christianson; p8 Jaggat /
Shutterstock.com; p9 (t) Shutterstock © Oskar
Calero, (b) © Foto Huebner/dpa/Corbis;
p10 3777190317 / Shutterstock.com; p11
(t) iStock © Richard Laurence, (b) cjmac
/ Shutterstock.com; p12 SÃ¡gi ElemÃ©r
/ Shutterstock.com; p13 Shutterstock ©
Vitaly Chernyshenko; p14 Michael Stokes /
Shutterstock.com; p15 Christopher Dodge
/ Shutterstock.com; p16 Max Earey /
Shutterstock.com; p17 (t) Shutterstock ©
Gravicapa, (b) Walter G Arce / Shutterstock.
com; p18 (t) Daimler AG, (b) iStock ©
acilo; p19 AFP/Getty Images; p20 AFP/
Getty Images; p21 (t) Shutterstock © JustAsc,
(b) iStock ©; p22 Daimler AG; p23 (t)
Shutterstock © Ben Smith, (b) 3777190317
/ Shutterstock.com; p24 Michael Stokes /
Shutterstock.com

Contents

Cars on the move

A car is a vehicle that runs on wheels. An engine burns fuel and provides the power to make the car's wheels go round. As the wheels turn, they move the car forward.

Bonnet panel with engine beneath

Cars are made up of thousands of parts. They are put together in a factory. The cars are tested to make sure they are safe to drive.

Wheel covered in a rubber tyre

ZOOM IN

Engines get hot from the fuel burning inside them. A spinning fan at the front of the engine forces air from outside over the engine to keep it cool.

Some cars, such as police cars, or those that are used by people with disabilities, can be adapted to suit the work that they do.

Boot for storage

FAST FACT

There are over 600 million cars being driven on roads all over the world.

Cars can be fitted with lifts to help people who use wheelchairs to get inside.

Get set, go!

A car journey begins when the driver starts the engine. A car needs a lot of power from its engine to start moving.

Cars pull away at the start of a race. The drivers try to get their car to go fast enough to take the lead.

FAST FACT

Some racing cars can go from standing still to 160 kilometres per hour in less than a second!

The driver uses a key to start the car's engine. When the engine starts, fuel pumps into it and is burned to generate power.

ZOOM IN

A car has different gears. A low gear is used when a car starts moving. It turns the car's wheels slowly but with great force. As the car speeds up the gears change, either automatically or by being controlled by the driver using the gear stick.

Steering a car

The driver controls how a car moves, turning left and right and travelling around corners or bends in the road. The driver uses a steering wheel to control the car's direction.

Crash helmet protects driver's head

Driver's hands grip the steering wheel

Engine

A racing kart has a small engine but, because it is light in weight, it can still travel fast. The driver has to steer the car quickly and accurately through all the different bends and turns on the track.

ZOOM IN

A car's steering wheel is connected to the front wheels. Turning the steering wheel in one direction moves the front wheels so that they point in the same direction.

Drivers slow their cars down as they turn into a bend. If a driver takes a corner too fast there is a risk that the car might spin out of control and leave the road or even flip over. The cars can speed up again as they leave the bend.

As these racing drivers enter a bend, they slow their cars down to keep them under control.

Driver number

Front wheels point right as the kart turns to the right

Bumper at front protects driver's feet

Staying on track

When things rub together they make a force called friction. This slows things down but it also provides grip. Car tyres use friction to grip the road or track.

The front and rear wings on a Formula One racing car create a force that presses the car down onto the track.

Driver sits in cockpit

Rear wing

Front wing

ZOOM IN

These racing tyres are kept warm in a heated blanket. Warmer tyres are stickier and grip the track better.

During a race, the tyres wear down and have to be replaced. The cars come off the track and into the pits, needing new tyres and more fuel. In a blur of action, workers finish these jobs in less than seven seconds!

Narrow body slices through air

Wide tyres grip track

During a pit stop, workers race to get a car back on the track as fast as possible.

Off-road driving

Some cars need to be able to leave smooth-surfaced roads and travel on muddy, sandy or snowy ground. These off-road cars are built to be tough as their journeys can be rough and very bumpy.

Wipers remove rain and dirt from the windscreen

Race number

FAST FACT

Every year, hundreds of vehicles take part in a cross-country race called the Dakar Rally. The race lasts three weeks!

A rally car sends up a cloud of dust as it races over rough ground during an off-road race.

ZOOM IN

Off-road cars have tyres with a chunky surface pattern. This helps them to grip the ground well.

Off-road cars have a frame of metal tubes inside them to make them stronger. This frame is called a roll cage. It protects the driver if the car rolls over onto its side or roof.

Co-driver helps keep the car on the right route

Powerful headlights for seeing through fog, dust storms and at night

Thick rubber tyres

Speeding up

To make a car go faster, a driver presses a foot pedal called the accelerator. This makes the engine work harder to turn the car's wheels more quickly.

Driver wears a crash helmet

Small front wheels guide the dragster along the track

Long, thin body slices through the air

This dragster racing car can travel at speeds of over 500km/h. A dragster race is run on a 403-metre-long straight piece of track. A race can last just five seconds!

The light on top of this French police car flashes as it speeds to the scene of a crime.

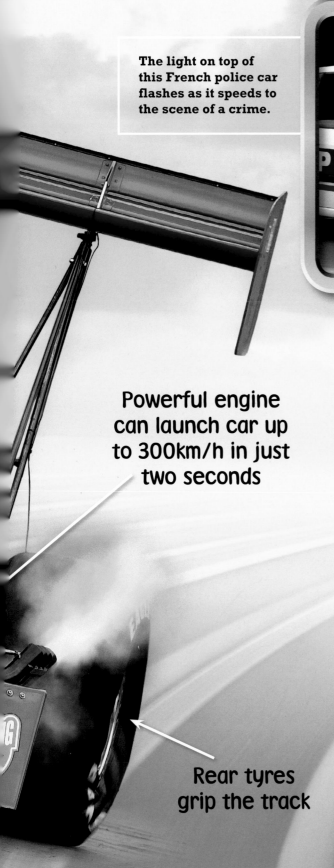

Powerful engine can launch car up to 300km/h in just two seconds

Rear tyres grip the track

Police cars often have to travel faster than other cars on the road. They use a flashing light and sound a siren to warn other road users that they are speeding past.

FAST FACT

The world's fastest police car is the Lamborghini Gallardo, which can reach a top speed of 309 km/h.

Slowing down

When drivers want to slow down or stop, they press the car's brake pedal. This makes brake pads press onto a disc inside each wheel. The rubbing of the pads on the discs creates friction, which slows down the car's wheels.

FAST FACT

The brakes in a Bugatti Veyron can slow the car down from 100km/h to standing still in less than two and a half seconds.

Brakes are fitted inside each wheel

Wheels turn round fast until brakes are used

ZOOM IN

When the brakes are used, brake lights at the back of the car shine red. This tells drivers behind that the car ahead is slowing down.

Car slows as it reaches a bend

Dragster racing cars travel so fast and have to stop so quickly, that ordinary brakes are not enough. Parachutes open behind a dragster and fill with air. This creates a force that pulls the car backwards. The force, known as drag, helps to slow the dragster down.

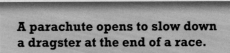

A parachute opens to slow down a dragster at the end of a race.

Different fuels

A car's engine needs fuel for it to work. Most engines use petrol or diesel fuels made from oil. When these fuels are burned in an engine, they can send harmful gases into the air. So scientists are working on other, cleaner ways of powering cars.

Low energy lights

ZOOM IN

When the battery pack runs down, the driver plugs the car into a recharging point.

Some cars fitted with electric motors get their electricity from sunlight. Solar panels on the car turn energy from the sun into electricity.

This strange looking car works with solar power.

electric drive

This Mercedes Fortwo car is driven by an electric motor. The motor gets electricity from a large battery pack stored inside the car.

Car seats driver and one passenger

Battery fitted in floor of car. Electric motor turns rear wheels (to drive the car forward)

FAST FACT

In 2004, a car powered by sunlight made a record-setting journey of 15,070 km across North America.

Driving safely

Cars are built and tested to keep the people who travel in them safe. When a new type of car is designed it is crashed in the lab to see how it will protect its driver and passengers. Experts study how the full-sized models of people, called crash test dummies, move around during the crash.

Dummy thrown forward by impact

Airbag

Front of cars crumple when they hit each other

Two cars are crashed together in a safety lab to find out what adjustments need to be made to improve car safety.

ZOOM IN

Seat belts stop you being forced forward in a crash and banging your head. Always fasten your seat belt when you travel in a car.

Forces from the crash are soaked up by the car's frame

An airbag inflates to stop the crash test dummy hitting the car's windscreen.

When a crash happens, airbags blow up like a balloon in a tiny fraction of a second. They cushion the driver and passenger's faces from injury.

Quiz

How much have you found out about cars at work? Try this quick quiz!

1. What part of a car keeps a driver and passengers in their seats?
a) roll cage
b) seat belt
c) airbag

2. What force helps brakes slow cars down?
a) drag
b) downforce
c) friction

3. Which foot pedal do drivers press to speed up a car?
a) brake
b) accelerator
c) clutch

4. Many electric cars store energy in what device?
a) a battery
b) gears
c) airbags

5. How long does the Dakar Rally last?
a) four days
b) one week
c) three weeks

6. If you turn a car's steering wheel to the left, which direction will the car go?
a) right
b) left
c) straight on

7. Many dragster races take how long from start to finish?
a) five seconds
b) two minutes
c) three hours

electric drive

Answers: 1.b, 2.c, 3.b, 4.a, 5.c, 6.b, 7.a

Glossary

accelerator a foot pedal which is pressed down to make the car go faster

battery a store of chemicals in a case which supplies electricity to parts of a car such as its lights

bonnet a body panel on a car that lifts up to reveal the engine

bumper a bar made of metal, plastic or rubber which stops damage to the car if it bumps into something

crash helmet a protective hat worn by racing car drivers to stop head injuries if they fall or have a crash

crash test dummy a figure that looks like a person used in testing to see how safe a vehicle is

engine the machinery that creates power to turn the car's wheels round

friction the force that slows movement between two objects which rub together

fuel petrol, diesel or another substance burned in an engine to create power to make a car move

karts small vehicles used for fun racing on race tracks

pit stop a break during a race when a car leaves the track for repairs, extra fuel or new tyres

roll cage a frame of metal tubes inside a car which protects people should the car topple over

solar panel a special panel that converts sunlight into electricity to power electric motors in a solar powered vehicle

steering controlling a car by making the wheels turn to go round bends

wings parts on racing cars and some sports cars which help press the car downwards so that it grips the track or ground

Further Information

Books

It's Amazing: Supercars, Annabel Savery, Franklin Watts, 2011
Machines on the Move: Cars, James Nixon, Franklin Watts, 2010
Ultimate Cars series, Rob Scott Colson, Wayland, 2009
Extreme Machines: Cars, David Jefferis, Franklin Watts, 2009
How Machines Work: Fast Cars, Ian Graham, Franklin Watts, 2008

Websites

http://www.funkidslive.com/features/fun-kids-guide-to-cars/
A fun guide to how the different parts of a car work.

http://www.explainthatstuff.com/carengines.html
How car engines work with lots of links to other facts about cars.

Places to Visit

The National Motor Museum, Brockenhurst, Hampshire, SO42 7ZN, UK
http://www.beaulieu.co.uk/attractions/national-motor-museum
This museum contains more than 200 cars including famous cars from TV and movies as well as a 1930s garage and lots of other exhibits.

Haynes International Motor Museum, Sparkford, Yeovil, Somerset, BA22 7LH, UK
http://www.haynesmotormuseum.com
More than 400 cars, from the early days of motoring to the latest sports cars, are on show at this fascinating museum.

Index

Katinka's Tail

Judith Kerr

HarperCollins *Children's Books*

For Ann-Janine,
with love and thanks

First published in hardback in Great Britain
by HarperCollins Children's Books in 2017
First published in paperback in 2018

10 9 8 7 6 5 4 3 2 1

ISBN: 978-0-00-825533-6

HarperCollins Children's Books is a division of HarperCollins Publishers Ltd.

Text and illustrations copyright © Kerr-Kneale Productions Ltd 2017

Visit our website at www.harpercollins.co.uk

Printed and bound in China

MIX
Paper from
responsible sources
FSC™ C007454

FSC
www.fsc.org

This book is produced from independently certified FSC™ paper
to ensure responsible forest management.

For more information visit: www.harpercollins.co.uk/green

This is my cat Katinka.
She is a lovely, perfectly ordinary pussycat.

People always notice Katinka.

Then some say, "That tail is really magic."

They say, "Look at that cat with the funny tail."

Others say, "What a peculiar cat. Is she peculiar in other ways too?" This makes me very cross, and I say, "She's just a lovely, perfectly ordinary pussycat."

First thing every morning
Katinka climbs up the
creeper…

to my bedroom window…

and when I draw back the curtains, there she is!

Sometimes she has been playing in the woods, and she is a bit grubby. Then I give her a nice brush.

But she won't let me brush her tail.

She knows that her tail is special.

She likes to help
me get dressed,

and always checks
my shoes for spiders.

Then we go down
to the kitchen.

Sometimes there is a dead
mouse on the floor…

or half a dead mouse.

I throw them out when Katinka isn't looking.

Then I give Katinka her breakfast.

But…

sometimes Katinka thinks my breakfast
looks more interesting.

Sometimes Katinka walks up the road with me.

She plays in the woods while I go to the shops.

But she is always there to meet me
when I come home…

and we unpack the shopping together.

Sometimes
Katinka does
a funny trick.
She lies on
the table.

Then she leans
over the edge...

and a bit more...

and a bit more…

until she
falls off.

Then I say,
"Oh, what a
clever pussycat!"
and she is
very pleased.

One night Katinka and I had
our supper.

Then I put her to bed in her basket…

and went to bed myself.

But in the middle of the night
I woke up with a big sneeze.

So I went downstairs
for some tissues.
Katinka's basket
was empty.

But then I saw her.
She was running,
and there was
something wrong
with her tail.

And the street was full of animals,
running after her.

And when they got to the woods, they all
disappeared, and I was alone in the dark.
But then I noticed a glow behind some trees,
and you'll never believe what I saw.
I shouted, "Katinka! What on earth are you
doing? Whatever are you doing with your tail?"

But Katinka just smiled and went on waving her tail, and then she suddenly floated up in the air, and so did all the animals, and so did I!

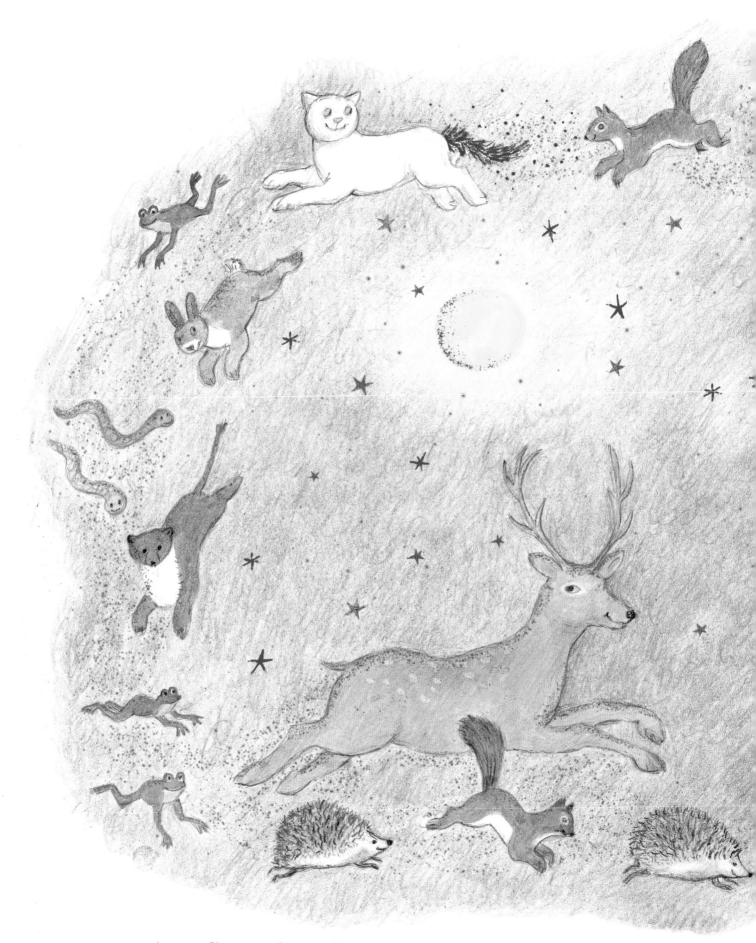

And we floated up through the clouds to the sky above,

and we flew round and round among the stars.

And then Katinka and I flew to
the moon…

and Katinka caught a
moon mouse and ate it.

And then I flew
back into my
bedroom,

and in the morning I woke up in my bed,
just as usual.
I thought, "What an amazing dream. I must
tell Katinka what I dreamt about her."

So I drew back the curtains, and there she was.
And I said, "Oh!"
Now, when people ask me about Katinka, I say,
"She's a lovely, perfectly ordinary pussycat."
And then I say, "Except, of course, for her tail."

BLÀTH

Carol Thompson

Tha mi toilicht', 's mi a tha,
fon a' phlaide bhrèagha bhlàth,

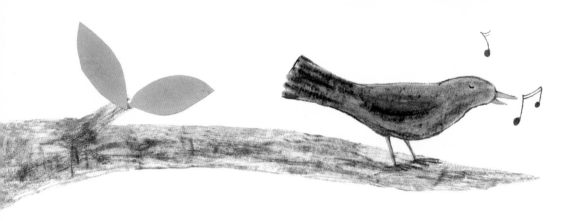

A' chiad fhoillseachadh sa Bheurla an 2011 le Child's Play (International) Ltd
Rathad Ashworth, Bridgemead, Swindon SN5 7YD

A' chiad fhoillseachadh sa Ghàidhlig 2012 le Acair Earranta, 7 Sràid Sheumais,
Steòrnabhagh, Eilean Leòdhais HS1 2QN

www.acairbooks.com
info@acairbooks.com

Chuidich Comhairle nan Leabhraichean am foillsichear le cosgaisean an leabhair seo.
Tha Acair a' faighinn taic bho Bhòrd na Gàidhlig.

Fhuair Urras Leabhraichean na h-Alba taic airgid bho Bhòrd na Gàidhlig
le foillseachadh nan leabhraichean Gàidhlig *Bookbug*

Clò-bhuailte ann an Heshan, Sìona
1 3 5 7 9 10 8 6 4 2

Gheibhear clàr catalogaidh dhen leabhar seo bho Leabharlann Bhreatainn.

ISBN 9780861523948

Blàth is seasgair le mo phlaide mar am famh a-staigh fon talamh.

Fon an t-sneachd tha lus a' fàs,
is an daolag air a shàil;
Seall, tha 'n dithis aca cho blàth.

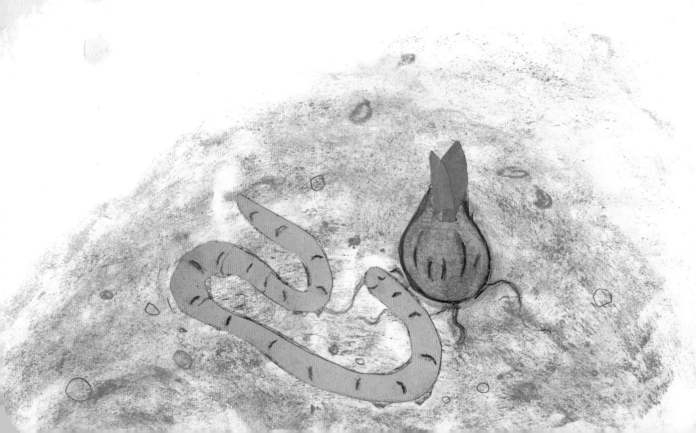

Cho seasgair ri bhith 'n nead nan eun,

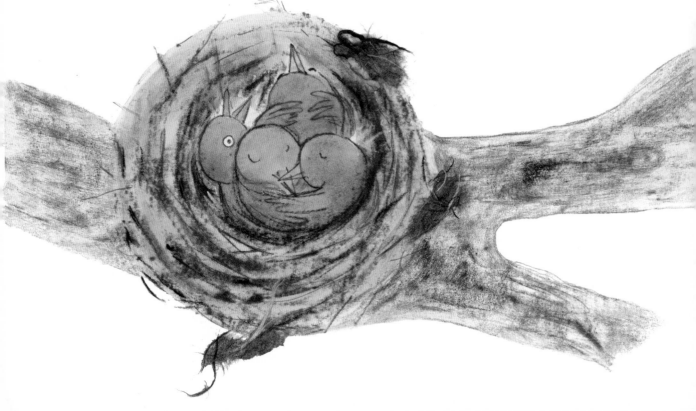

Tha a' mhuc cho blàth le còt'
mu meadhan.

A bheil an t-seilcheag
blàth is sunndach,
is i na cadal anns a' pholl sin?

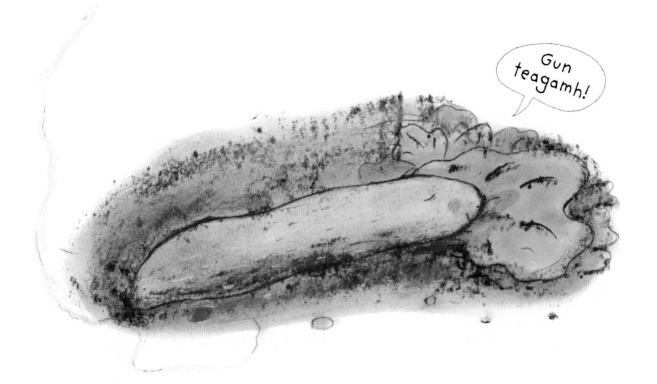

Tha leabaidh
sheasgair càilear blàth
mar am peasair
's e ri fàs!

Seilcheag
bheag bhlàth,
cruinn mar
bàlla beag
snàth,

Luchag bheag dhòigheil
cho blàth staigh na seòmar.

Madadh-allaidh na chadal
le socais bhoban mu chasan —
feadhainn bhlàth rinn a Ghranaidh,

Cho blàth is seasgair ri cat
na shìneadh air mat.

Cudail blàth
gaolach ...

An rud AS FHEÀRR
air an t-saoghal!